P9-CKG-652

PRESENTATION

To _____

From _____

Date _____

World Inspirational Books

AN ORIGINAL

GENERAL EDITOR, *David A. MacLennan*

THE WISDOM OF THE PSALMS

Selections and expositions
based on Commentary by John Calvin

BY WILLIAM F. KEESECKER

The World Publishing Company
NEW YORK AND CLEVELAND

Published by The World Publishing Company

Published simultaneously in Canada by Nelson, Foster & Scott Ltd.

First printing—1970

Copyright © 1970 by The World Publishing Company

All rights reserved

Library of Congress catalog card number: 79-1311564

Printed in the United States of America

WORLD PUBLISHING

TIMES MIRROR

NEW YORK AND CLEVELAND

ACKNOWLEDGMENTS

Special acknowledgement is made to the following for permission to reprint selections from books and periodicals:

ABINGDON PRESS: *A Treasury of Sermon Illustrations.* Charles L. Wallis. Abingdon Press, Nashville, 1949. *The Wind of the Spirit.* James S. Stewart. Abingdon Press, Nashville and Hodder & Stoughton Ltd., London, 1968. Reprinted by permission.

ASSOCIATION PRESS: *Treasury of the Christian Faith.* Stanley I. Stuber and Thomas C. Clark. Association Press, New York, 1949.

BOARD OF EVANGELISM AND SOCIAL SERVICE: *This Is Our Faith.* John Dow. Board of Evangelism and Social Service, United Church of Canada, Toronto, 1943.

THE CHRISTIAN CENTURY FOUNDATION: *The Role of the Residential Parish Church in the Inner City* by Walter E. Ziegenhals in *The Pulpit* issue of June 1969, Copyright 1969 by Christian Century Foundation, and a poem by James L. Stone in *The Pulpit* issue of March 1960, Copyright 1960 by Christian Century Foundation. Reprinted by permission.

DOUBLEDAY & COMPANY, INC.: *A Rumor of Angels.* Peter Berger. Doubleday & Company, Garden City, New York, 1969.

WM. B. EERDMANS PUBLISHING COMPANY: *Commentaries on the Psalms.* John Calvin. 5 vols. Copyright 1949 by Wm. B. Eerdmans Publishing Company, Grand Rapids, Michigan. All quotes are used by permission.

HARPER & ROW, PUBLISHERS: *A Calvin Treasury.* William F. Keesecker. Harper and Row, New York, 1961; *Pastoral Counselling.* Carroll A. Wise. Harper and Row, New York, 1961; *The Inward Journey.* Howard Thurman. Harper and Row, New York, 1961; *To Conquer Loneliness.* Harold B. Walker. Harper and Row, New York, 1966.

HOUGHTON MIFFLIN COMPANY: *Churchill Taken From the Diaries of Lord Moran.* Houghton Mifflin, New York, 1966.

THE MACMILLAN COMPANY: *Mere Christianity.* C. S. Lewis. The Macmillan Company, New York, 1952.

NATIONAL COUNCIL OF THE CHURCHES OF CHRIST IN THE U.S.A.: Scripture quotations are from the *Revised Standard Version Bible,* copyright 1946 and 1952 by the Division of Christian Education of the National Council of the Churches of Christ in the U.S.A. Used by permission.

PRESBYTERIAN BOARD OF PUBLICATION: *Calvin's Institutes.* ed. by John Allen. Presbyterian Board of Publication, Philadelphia, 1813.

SIMON AND SCHUSTER INC.: *The Lessons Of History.* Will and Ariel Durant. Reprinted by permission of Simon and Schuster, New York, 1968.

WESTMINSTER PRESS: *A Serious Call to a Devout and Holy Life.* William Law. Westminster Press, Philadelphia, 1948; *Early Christian Fathers,* ed. by C. C. Richardson. Vol. I. Westminster Press, Philadelphia, 1953; *Institutes of the Christian Religion.* ed. by John T. McNeil. Westminster Press, Philadelphia, 1960.

Introduction to John Calvin

ONE OF THE most complex of personalities, as he was one of the most influential thinkers of many centuries, John Calvin is a difficult man to introduce. This leader of the sixteenth century Protestant Reformation has been praised as one of the greatest Christian teachers since the Apostle Paul and defamed as a destroyer of much that was good in the great church in which he was born and trained. Many Protestants, including clergymen, think of him as a kind of sanctimonious character "with horns and wreathed about with the incense of brimstone." There has been both an irrational aversion to him and at times an unrealistic adulation of him. John Calvin (Jean Calvin in French) was neither demon nor divine. He was a human being of intellectual powers, creative capacity and devotion to God rarely equalled in our human story.

Born in 1509 in Noyon, France, he was the son of a notary who had what has been called "advantageous connections." At the age of 14 John Calvin was sent to the University of Paris, with his parents' hope that he would prepare for the priesthood. He did further study in Orleans and Bourges for the practice of law. Little is known of his spiritual pilgrimage until his twenty-fifth year. In 1558 he wrote of this period: "God by a sudden conversion subdued my heart to teachableness."

Calvin's conversion impelled him to devote intense and continuous study of the Bible as a source of authority for the Christian life and for the Church. He rejected the old order of the church under the papacy but he remained a high churchman in holding a high doctrine of the Holy Catholic Church which is invisible and embraces all Christians.

This scholarly man with an astonishing ability to produce religious literature was soon called to join the other great leader of the Reformation, Martin Luther, to bear the burden of leadership. Calvin undertook many practical duties in Geneva. As an American historian, John T. McNeill, recently wrote, "At the price of great effort amid tasks of teaching, preaching, counseling and controversy, he maintained a high standard of excellence in his writings with respect to knowledge, argumentation and style." Although there are occasional lapses into vituperation against his opponents, reading any of his works convinces most readers that Calvin's one absorbing passion was to glorify the great, sovereign God whose faithful servant he sought always to be. Calvin's published works fill fifty-nine volumes, and others, mainly sermons, are being added. His most famous work, *The Institutes of the Christian Religion*, is a monumental theological work and explains why he is called the theologian of protestantism and the founder of Presbyterianism. Calvin was married, and became the father of one child who died in infancy. That he was far from the ogre many have considered him to be may be judged by his pastoral ministry to many individuals in Geneva and elsewhere. Also, his commentary on Bible books such as the Psalms, portray a sincere, devoted lover of God and of Jesus Christ through whom God's redemptive love acted so wonderfully.

This very limited selection of passages from Calvin's commentary on the Old Testament Psalms may well show the faith which led him to choose the personal crest he did. This pictures a flaming heart upon an open outstretched hand offered up to God. The motto reads, "My heart I give Thee, Lord, eagerly and entirely."

THE AUTHOR

The Reverend Dr. William F. Keesecker, pastor of Grace United Presbyterian Church, Wichita, Kansas, is a scholarly preacher of the Christian gospel. He makes no pretension to being an authority on John Calvin or an expert interpreter of Calvinism. Nevertheless, Dr. Keesecker, graduate of the College of Emporia, McCormick Theological Seminary, Chicago, with graduate work at Union Theological Seminary, New York City, has become an authority and interpreter although he would claim only amateur standing. He published *A Calvin Treasury* (Harper & Row, 1961). As readers of these pages will discover, he writes felicitously and is singularly gifted in relating John Calvin and biblical literature to contemporary writers and situations. In a very helpful sense this little volume is a Commentary by Keesecker on Calvin's Commentary on the Psalms. It will provide intellectual stimulus and spiritual resource for daily living.

David A. MacLennan
General Editor

PROSPERITY

Psalm 1:3 "He is like a tree planted by streams of water, that yields its fruit in its season, and its leaf does not wither. In all that he does, he prospers."

The things that matter most to us did not matter at all to Jesus Christ. He had little time for that upon which we place highest value, namely, possessions, prestige and power. Why was he able to resist the glittering idols of the human mind and heart? When he had the chance to have them all (Matt. 4:1-12), why did he turn them down? John Calvin gives the clue:

"The Psalmist here (1:3) . . . shows in what respect those who fear God are to be accounted happy, namely, not because they enjoy an evanescent and empty gladness, but because they are in a desirable condition. There is in the words an implied contrast between the figure of a tree planted in a situation well watered, and the decayed appearance of one which, although it may flourish beautifully for a time, yet soon withers on account of the barrenness of the soil in which it is placed. . . . The ungodly . . . have such an overflowing abundance of wealth and honors, that nothing seems wanting to their present happiness . . . yet, having no root in the ground, nor even a sufficiency of moisture from which they may derive nourishment, the whole of their beauty by and by disappears, and withers away. It is, therefore, the blessing of God alone which preserves any in a prosperous condition."

Christ calls us to a prosperity of soul which springs not from what we own but from what owns us. He calls us to repentance, and forgiveness, to right intention, to ardent prayer, to irresistible love. These create the "prosperous condition" which is the true blessing of God.

Prayer: Keep us, O God, from losing the things money cannot buy. In Christ's name. Amen.

SOLITUDE

Psalm 4:4 "Be angry, but sin not; commune with your own hearts on your beds, and be silent."

A person is never farther from being a Christian than when he seeks to escape life's responsibilities, irritations and burdens. Solitude which deliberately avoids human involvement so as to concentrate on personal concerns is self-centered and self-defeating.

There is, however, a solitude spoken of by the Psalmist which renews the soul and invigorates the spirit. John Calvin wrote of it as follows:

"To commune upon one's bed, is a form of expression taken from the common practice and experience of men. We know that, during our contacts with men in the daytime, our thoughts are distracted, and we often judge rashly, being deceived by the external appearance; whereas in solitude, we can give to any subject a closer attention; and, farther, the sense of shame does not then hinder a man from thinking about disguise of his own faults. . . . David, therefore, exhorts his enemies to withdraw from those who witnessed and judged of their actions on the public stage of life, and to be alone, that they may examine themselves more truthfully and honestly. This exhortation has a respect to us all . . . for there is nothing to which men are more prone than to deceive one another with empty applause, until each man enters into himself, and communes alone with his own heart."

> Set aside a day or two
>   Now and then to be alone,
> Hours when visions you renew,
>   When your soul is all your own.

Prayer: O God, nerve us to dare to have solitude so that we may face thee, find others and see ourselves honestly. Amen.

Psalm 5:11a "But let all who take refuge in thee rejoice, let them ever sing for joy."

What is joy? One might answer that it is celebration. The Prodigal Son who wanted to be free, and whose quest led him into a far country, there to express his freedom, knew joy. Yet his joyful liberty ended up as license. Another might say that joy lies in the feeling of mastery which comes when one overcomes opposition, defies defeat, surmounts obstacles and achieves a coveted goal in the face of great opposition. Yet to attain mastery only leaves one longing for more worlds to conquer. Still another may say that joy is fulfillment. To marry, to know the birth of a child, to work and come to terms with death, this is to experience joy. Yet even to successfully cope with the common ventures of marriage, birth, work and death leaves one still earthbound.

Calvin wrote, ". . . true joy procedes from no other source than from the protection of God. We may be exposed to a thousand deaths, but this one consideration ought abundantly to suffice us, that we are covered and defended by the hand of God. And this will be the case, if the main shadows of this world cannot so beguile us as to excite us to take shelter under them."

Christian joy comes as we assign ourselves over to the great God who cleanses, forgives, makes us whole and keeps that which we have committed unto him against any evil day. William Law wrote, "It is certain that whatever seeming calamity happens to you, if you thank and praise God for it, you turn it into a blessing. . . . [The thankful spirit] turns all that it touches into happiness."

Prayer: Eternal Father, help us to keep thee at the center of life, that we may accept every experience as thy training for better things than we can understand. So shall we find joy. In Christ's name. Amen.

INQUIRY

Psalm 10:3-4 "For the wicked boasts of the desires of his heart, and the man greedy for gain curses and re-

nounces the Lord. In the pride of his countenance the wicked does not seek him; all his thoughts are, 'There is no God.'"

From the beginning man has sought to acquire knowledge. In spite of the fact that his inquiries have been corrupted by an overweening pride which perverts judgment and distorts truth, man still goes on seeking to attain more and more knowledge, believing that it is the source of his life as a person; that it lifts him out of savagery and that it produces culture.

Honorus, a pupil of Anselm, once wrote, "The exile of men is ignorance; their homeland wisdom, and the way thither passes through the several cities of the arts, science, and the philosophies."

Though he lived in a prescientific age, Calvin was a modern in that he stressed inquiry. He wrote: "The beginning of well-doing in a man's life is inquiry; in other words, we can only begin to do well when we keep ourselves from following, without choice and discrimination, the dictates of our own fancy, and from being carried away by the wayward propensities of our flesh." Then the Genevan reformer sagely cautions: "But the exercise of inquiring proceeds from humility, when we assign to God, as is reasonable, the place of judge and ruler over us."

Prayer: Keep us, O God, aware of the pain, sweat, toil and tears that lie behind the heritage of our culture. Keep in us a growing edge that we may not live unthinkingly in today's world. Above all, give us the awareness of thyself as the source of our knowledge, so that we may depart from evil and find true understanding. In Christ's name. Amen.

PATIENCE

Psalm 11:5 "The Lord tests the righteous and the wicked, and his soul hates him that loves violence."

John Calvin held that the patient man derives his patience from a fundamental trust in the ultimate decency of things. He wrote: "When . . . deceit, graft, treachery, cruelty, violence, and extortion reign in the world; in short, when all things are thrown into disorder and darkness by injustice and wickedness, let faith serve as a lamp to enable us to behold God's heavenly throne, and let that sight suffice to make us wait in patience for the restoration of things to a better state.

" 'What is faith?' cried Tertullian in the third century, and answered his own question: 'Faith is patience with the lamp lit.' That is a lovely word, worth inscribing on the front page of your private Bible. For this is where the Christian has the stoic and the cynic and the fatalist utterly and forever beaten. Patience is stoic: patience with the lamp lit is Christian. The stoic may talk grimly about taking fate by the throat; the cynic may shrug his shoulders and say he 'couldn't care less.' But it is a different trumpet-note you meet on every page of the New Testament. Here are men, to use their own words, 'glorying in tribulation,' 'enduring longsuffering with joyfulness.' Here is not only 'Praise to the Holiest in the height,' here is also 'And in the depth be praise!' "

> Not so in haste my heart!
> Have faith in God and wait;
> Although he linger long
> He never comes too late.

Prayer: Give us patience, O God, which is the gift of thy grace. Teach us to believe because thou hast first empowered us to believe. Help us to know that thou dost love us with an everlasting love. Amen.

UNITY

Psalm 15:1a "O Lord, who shall sojourn in thy tent?"

John Calvin was a strong advocate of church unity. He clearly recognized that there could not be two churches of Christ, nor four, nor eight nor one hundred and sixty, nor three hundred and twenty. He knew that men can and do fracture and weaken the visible unity of Christ's church by their sinfulness. "We too often see the Church of God defaced by much impurity," he wrote. But he also clearly recognized that the church is one in spite of what men do. "When the temple of God happens to be tainted by many impurities, we may not contract such disgust and chagrin as will make us withdraw from it. By impurities I understand the vices of a corrupt and polluted life." Calvin did not condone unholy living. "If we really wish to be reckoned among the number of the children of God, the Holy Ghost teaches us, that we must show ourselves to be such by a holy and an upright life; for it is not enough to serve God by outward ceremonies, unless we also live uprightly, and without doing wrong to our neighbors."

Nevertheless, Calvin held the basis of church unity to be doctrinal. "Provided religion continue pure as to doctrine and worship, we must not be so much stimulated at the faults and sins which man commit, as on that account to rend the unity of the church." A luminous body of commonly held Christian convictions which has all the richness of the Christian revelation is the only basis for church unity. Such doctrine enables the church not only to satisfy the intellectual needs of her members, but to outlive the paganisms of the day and give meaning and purpose to living.

Prayer: Help us, O Lord, to passionately believe, yet be compassionate; to have burning convictions and yet to be winsomely tolerant, for the sake of the great Head of the church, even Jesus Christ. Amen.

CREATION

Psalm 19:1a "The heavens are telling the glory of God."

"David shows how it is that the heavens proclaim to us the glory of God, namely by openly bearing testimony that they have not been put together by chance, but were wonderfully created by the supreme Architect. When we behold the heavens, we cannot but be elevated, by the contemplation of them, to Him who is their great Creator; and the beautiful arrangement and wonderful variety which distinguish the courses and station of the heavenly bodies, together with the beauty and splendor which are manifest in them, cannot but furnish us with an evident proof of His providence."

In the not too distant past Calvin's ascription of praise to the Creator would have been considered to be somewhat archaic, for science was locked in a materialistic mold which regarded creation as being the result of self-origination in which no Divine will or hand was to be seen. C. S. Lewis describes the viewpoint as follows: "Matter and space just happen to exist, and always have existed, nobody knows why; and . . . matter, behaving in certain fixed ways, has just happened, by a sort of fluke, to produce creatures like ourselves who are able to think. By one chance in a thousand something hit our sun and made it produce the planets; and by another thousandth chance the chemicals necessary for life, and the right temperature, occurred on one of these planets, and so some of the matter on this earth came alive; and then, by a very long series of changes, the living creatures developed into things like us."

Today we can no longer accept a closed, mechanistic view of creation. Science suggests that mass and energy are the same thing viewed in different ways. Also, time and space lose their distinguishing identities in the vast, fathomless depths of the outer cosmos. Puny man, handicapped by his insufficient conceptions and locked in the cell of his senses, can only move stumblingly through the dimness of the reality he confronts, whether it be in the rudimentary specks glimpsed through the microscope, or in the boundless universe of time and space seen by the telescope. Whether he ever pierces deeper into the depths below or the heights above remains to be seen, for as the Apostle Paul wrote, "for we know in part, and we prophesy in part . . . we see through a glass, darkly; . . ." (I Cor. 13:9, 11. KJV)

Calvin sounds strangely modern: "As soon as we acknowledge God to be the supreme Architect, who has erected the beauteous fabric of the universe, our minds must necessarily be ravished with wonder at his infinite goodness, wisdom, and power."

Prayer: Teach us, O God, to see nature as the revelation of thy faithfulness. Instill in us the confidence that thou dost inspire every promise thou dost implant, and every trust thou dost invoke, through Jesus Christ our Lord. Amen.

Psalm 22:1a *"My God, my God, why hast thou for-saken me?"*

"As our Saviour Jesus Christ, when hanging on the cross, and when ready to yield up his soul into the hands of God his Father, made use of these very words (Matt. 27:46b), we must consider how these two things can agree, that Christ was the only begotten Son of God, and that yet he was so penetrated with grief, seized with so great mental trouble, as to cry out that God his Father had forsaken him. The apparent contradiction between these two statements has constrained many interpreters to have recourse to evasions for fear of charging Christ with blame in this matter. Accordingly, they have said that Christ made this complaint rather according to the opinion of the common people, who witnessed his sufferings, than from any feeling which he had of being deserted by his Father. But they have not considered that they greatly lessen the benefit of our redemption, in imagining that Christ was altogether exempted from the terrors which the judgment of God strikes into sinners. . . . As he became our representative, and took upon him our sins, it was certainly necessary that he should appear before the judgment-seat of God as a sinner. From this proceeded the terror and dread which constrained him to pray for deliverance from death; not that it was so grievous to him merely to depart from this life; but because there was before his eyes the curse of God, to which all who are sinners are exposed."

Glad are those who in their grief turn to Christ, for they shall find in him an ally, a friend, a presence to comfort them and send them on their way better disciples, concerned about Christ's cause in the world.

Prayer: Our Father, wilt thou warm all hearts that are cold because of sorrow over past sin. May thy love flow through us and through the one perfect sacrifice of Jesus Christ enable us to find help in our time of need. Amen.

Psalm 24:3-4a "Who shall ascend the hill of the Lord? And who shall stand in his holy place? He who has clean hands and a pure heart."

What is it to be pure in heart? Is it not to be single minded? Is it not to think the same way, to exhibit the same side of one's nature, to speak with the same integrity today and tomorrow? To be pure in heart is to have a will single in purpose, and to react in a manner commensurate with one's conviction.

Calvin wrote, "True purity, no doubt, has its seat in the heart, but it manifests its fruits in the works of the hands. The Psalmist, therefore, very properly joins to a pure heart the purity of the whole life; for that man acts a ridiculous part who boasts of having a sound heart, if he does not show by his fruits that the root is good. On the other hand, it will not suffice to frame the hands, feet, and eyes, according to the rule of righteousness, unless purity of heart precede outward continence."

Jesus said, "Blessed are the pure in heart, for they shall see God" (Matt. 5:8). How? When one concentrates on "Whatever is true, whatever is honorable, whatever is just, whatever is pure, whatever is lovely, whatever is gracious, . . ." (Phil. 4:8) then light comes to dispel the darkness of doubt; the positive replaces the negative in one's outlook, and good works put evil to rout.

When Tennyson was once asked what was his dearest wish, he answered, "A clearer vision of God." When we will deliberately seek whatever strengthens reason, ennobles conscience, makes clearer our understanding of God and creates a relish for things spiritual we will be admitted into the presence of the Most High.

Prayer: "Make me a captive Lord, and then I shall be free;
Force me to render up my sword, and I shall conqueror be,

I sink in life's alarms when myself I stand;
Imprison me within thine arms, and strong shall be my hand." Amen.
(George Matheson, 1842-1906.)

FEAR

Psalm 27:1a "The Lord is my light and my salvation; whom shall I fear?"

To be human is to know fear. Whether one lives in the terror-ridden jungle of an underdeveloped nation, or in the locked-in security of the city high-rise apartment, apprehension is a companion of the way. "It is impossible to look round on the strange aspect of all things—the church reeling to her center with conflicting opinions; in all circles whether political or religious, minds unsettled and anticipating a crisis; men's hearts failing them for fear, and for looking for those things which are coming upon earth—without feeling that our path will be a rugged one, and that the hour of trial is at hand." These words, so contemporary in meaning, were written during the middle of the last century by one of England's foremost preachers, F. W. Robertson. Fear afflicts every age.

How can we deal with fear? Calvin urged the identification of the source of fear: "Certainly we find that all our fears arise from this source, that we are too anxious about our life, while we acknowledge not that God is its preserver. We can have no tranquillity, therefore, until we attain the persuasion that our life is sufficiently guarded, because it is protected by His omnipotent power. . . . Let us learn, therefore, to put such a value on God's power to protect us as to put to flight all our fears. Not that the minds of the faithful can, by reason of the infirmity of the flesh, be at all time entirely devoid of fear; but immediately recovering courage, let us, from the high power of our confidence, look down upon all our dangers with contempt."

Jesus believed in a God who because of his love for men would seek to work life out to the very best possible advantage for every individual. This was his abiding faith. When we recognize that deliverance from the demonic fear is more than a Band-Aid operation and put our faith in him who alone is able to "keep us from falling," we then will no longer have to be afraid.

Prayer: Living Lord—there is a knowledge
That comes from revelation to those who believe.
There is no need for the individual to live
In the fear of doubt. We can say with Job:
"I know that my Redeemer liveth."
Strengthen this certainty in us. Amen.

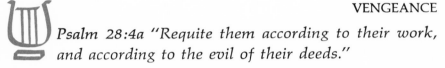

VENGEANCE

Psalm 28:4a "Requite them according to their work, and according to the evil of their deeds."

"Before a man can, therefore, denounce vengeance against the wicked, he must first shake himself free from all improper feelings in his own mind. In the second place, prudence must be exercised, that the heinousness of the evils which offend us drive us not to intemperate zeal, which happened even to Christ's disciples, when they desired that fire might be brought from heaven to consume those who refused to entertain their Master" (Luke 9:54). In particular, we must observe this general rule, that we cordially desire and labor for the welfare of the whole human race."

Vindictive passion is one of the ugliest faults in human nature. Its perverseness lies in two areas according to John Calvin: First, revenge arouses the improper feeling of judgment of others. We desire to hurt another by making him condemn some fault of his own. Thus, one judges another by his own standard rather than on the basis of what God in Christ wants for him. 'Judge not, that you be not judged,' said Jesus (Matt. 7:1). Secondly, revenge drives us to intemperate zeal in our effort to make the evil of the bad man to be to him what it is to everyone else. We want the guilty party to suffer, to know that we want him to suffer and to be aware that he is suffering at our hands.

One gets rid of resentment, according to Calvin, when he labors for the good of "the whole human race." One way this is accomplished is to get angry with the monstrous evils of the world and not misdirect our anger toward persons who happen to be the instruments of evil. The Christian hates the sin but loves the sinner. In so doing he keeps the poison of revenge from destroying the health of his world, his community and himself.

Prayer: O God, help us to banish resentment that we may sincerely pray, "Forgive us our debts as we forgive our debtors." In the name of the compassionate Christ we pray. Amen.

SCIENCE

Psalm 29:3 "The voice of the Lord is upon the waters; the God of glory thunders, the Lord, upon many waters."

"What a monstrous thing it is, that while all the irrational portion of the creation tremble before God, men alone, who are endued with sense and reason, are not moved! Moreover, though they possess genius and learning, they employ enchantments to shut their ears against God's voice, however powerful, lest it should reach their hearts. Philosophers think not that they have reasoned skillfully enough about inferior causes, unless they separate God very far from his works. It is a diabolical science, however, which fixes our contemplations on the works of nature, and turns them away from God. If anyone who wished to know a man should take no notice of his face, but should fix his eyes only on the points of his nails, his folly might justly be derided. But far greater is the folly of those philosophers, who, out of mediate and proximate causes, weave themselves veils, lest they should be compelled to acknowledge the hand of God, which manifestly displays itself in his works.

"But nothing is more preposterous than, when we meet with mediate causes, however many, to be stopped and retarded by them, as by so many obstacles, from approaching God; for this is the same as if a man were to remain at the very rudiments of things during his whole life, without going farther. In short, this is to learn in such a manner that you can never know anything. That shrewdness alone, therefore, is worthy of praise, which elevates us by these means even to heaven, in order that not a confused noise only may strike our ears, but that the voice of the Lord may penetrate our hearts, and teach us to pray and serve God."

Prayer: Help us, our Father, to rediscover the truth that the road to hell is paved with good intentions. Give us the vision to see that unless our scientific genius is directed toward the highest human good it will hinder rather than help mankind. Great and marvelous are thy works, O God. May our use of them help bring peace to the world. Amen.

HOPE

Psalm 31:1a "In thee, O Lord, do I seek refuge."

"[The Psalmist] held it as a principle, that the hope which depends upon God cannot possibly be disappointed. . . ." As Will and Ariel Durant in *The Lessons of History* wrote:

"In the debate between ancients and moderns it is not at all clear that the ancients carry off the prize. Shall we count it a trivial achievement that famine has been eliminated in modern states, and that one country can now grow enough food to overfeed itself and yet send hundreds of millions of bushels of wheat to nations in need? Are we ready to scuttle the science that has so diminished superstition, obscurantism, and religious intolerance, or the technology that has spread food, home ownership, comfort, education, and leisure beyond any precedent? Would we really prefer the Athenian agora or the Roman comitia to the British Parliament or the United States Congress, or be content under a narrow franchise like Attica's or the selection of rulers by a praetorian guard? Would we rather have lived under the laws of the Athenian Republic or the Roman Empire than under constitutions that give us habeas corpus, trial by jury, religious and intellectual freedom, and the emancipation of women? Are our morals, lax through they are, worse than those of the ambisexual Alcibiades, or has any American President imitated Pericles, who lived with a learned courtesan? Are we ashamed of our great universities, our many publishing houses, our bountiful public libraries? There were great dramatists in Athens, but was any greater than Shakespeare, and was Aristophanes as profound and humane as Molière? Was the oratory of Demosthenes, Isocrates, and Aeschines superior to that of Chatham, Burke, and Sheridan? Shall we place Gibbon below Herodotus or Thucydides? Is there anything in ancient prose fiction comparable to the scope and depth of the modern novel? We may grant the superiority of the ancients in art, though some of us might still prefer Notre Dame de Paris to the Parthenon. If the Founding Fathers of the United States could return to America, or Fox and Bentham to England, or Voltaire and Diderot to France, would they not reproach us as ingrates for our blindness to our good fortune in living today and not yesterday—not even under Pericles or Augustus?

"We should not be greatly disturbed by the probability that our civilization will die like any other. As Frederick asked his retreating troops at Kolin, 'Would you live forever?' Perhaps it is desirable that life should take fresh forms, that new civilizations and centers should have their turn. Meanwhile the effort to meet the challenge of the rising East may reinvigorate the West."

Calvin wrote: "Oh! that all of us would practice it [hope] in such a manner as that, whenever we approach to God, we may be able with David to declare that our prayers proceed from this source, namely, from a firm persuasion that our safety depends on the power of God."

Prayer: O God, when it comes to hope may our shelves not be bare. Give us a firm persuasion that our safety depends upon thee. Amen.

MUSIC

Psalm 33:2-3 "Praise the Lord with the lyre, make melody to him with the harp of ten strings! Sing to him a new song, play skillfully on the strings, with loud shouts."

Very likely John Calvin would have preferred to have the organ and the church choir in the balcony—out of sight! It was not that he was tone deaf or disdained music as such, but rather that he wanted to avoid any ostentatious display of human artistry that might divert man's attention from his objective in worship, namely, to glorify God.

"It is evident that the Psalmist here expressed the vehement and ardent affection which the faithful ought to have in praising God, when he enjoins musical instruments to be employed for this purpose. He would have nothing omitted by believers which tends to animate the minds and feelings of men in singing God's praises. . . . God, no doubt, can, properly speaking, be celebrated only by the articulate voice; but it is not without reason that David adds to this those aids by which believers were wont to stimulate themselves the more to this exercise. . . . I have no doubt that playing upon cymbals, touching the harp and the viol, and all that kind of music, which is so frequently mentioned in the Psalms, was a part of the education; that is to say, the puerile instruction of the law. . . . Instruments should, I think, make it their object not to dissever their cheerfulness from the praises of God. . . . Does anyone object, that music is very useful for awakening the minds of men and moving their hearts? I own it; but we should always take care that no corruption creep in, which might both defile the pure worship of God and involve men in superstition."

We sing and play so that God may hear and be pleased. He is the Author of life and he is the Master Composer whose music flows through the men he has inspired. Let us rejoice in the gift of music and sing to the glory of God.

Prayer: O God, may our music direct our minds and hearts to thee, that amid the discordant sounds of our strident age we may know that thy sure direction and purpose are holding life together. In Christ's name. Amen.

PEACE

Psalm 34:14 "Depart from evil, and do good; seek peace, and pursue it."

"[The Psalmist] teaches us not merely that we ought to seek peace, but if at any time it shall seem to flee from us, he bids us use our every effort without ceasing in pursuing it. This, however, must be understood with some limitation. It will often happen, that when good and humble men have done everything in their power to secure peace, so far from softening the hearts of the wicked, or inclining them to uprightness, they rather excite their malice. Their impiety, also, often constrains us to separate from them, and to avoid them; nay, when they defy God, by proclaiming, as it were, open war against him, it would be disloyalty and treason on our part not to oppose and resist them. But here David means only that in our own personal affairs we should be meek and condescending, and endeavor, as far as in us lies, to maintain peace, though its maintenance should prove to us a source of such trouble and inconvenience."

The real peace of God is not an experience which man does or gives to himself, but is rather the result of a relationship with God which restores and produces a sense of equilibrium within the personality, and between the person and his world. As such, it involves all the processes of personality. As Carroll Wise has written, "It is not a condition of absence of conflict, but a deep sense of unity and fellowship which enables a person to handle conflicts creatively."

Prayer: Teach us anew, our Father, that real peace is not so much a matter of strategy as it is of sainthood. Help us to get our priorities straight so that we may seek first thy kingdom and so open the door to peace. In Christ's name. Amen.

CONSCIENCE

Psalm 35:11-12 "Malicious witnesses rise up; they ask me of things that I know not. They requite me evil for good; my soul is forlorn."

It is generally acknowledged that man has a conscience and that the conscience serves a useful purpose. Winston Churchill wrote, "The only guide to a man is his conscience; the only shield to his memory is the rectitude and sincerity of his actions. It is very imprudent to walk through life without this shield. . . ."

Calvin was aware of the cardinal role played by conscience. He asserted, "In old times, it was a common proverb among the heathen, 'There is no theatre more beautiful than a good conscience;' and in this they uttered a noble sentiment; . . ." Yet, Calvin knew that while the conscience tells one to do right it does not tell him what is right. Therefore, he wrote, "No man can be sustained and supported by the purity of his conscience unless he has recourse to God." Through the Word of God contained in the Scriptures; but more especially through the Word made flesh in Jesus Christ, the conscience is educated. Calvin felt that conscience functioned as "An internal witness and monitor of the duties we owe to God, shows us the difference between good and evil and accuses us when we deviate from our duty."

Prayer: Grant us the courage, O Lord, to follow conscience, even when it is difficult to do so. Even more, we beseech thee, grant us the desire to rightly form conscience through testing it by the universal norms of man's unchanging nature and thine own nature itself. In Christ's name. Amen.

ANXIETY

Psalm 37:18 "The Lord knows the days of the blameless, and their heritage will abide for ever."

Anxiety arises when one's basic values are threatened. When a person feels that the inner citadel of his being is in danger of being overwhelmed, then he is anxious. If one were to try to identify the dominant cause of anxiety in our age he might well settle upon meaninglessness. The specter that our lives are ultimately worthless, our decisions futile and all our goals illusory may well be the chief reason for the feeling of emptiness so widespread in our time. Is there some good news from God which can fill our emptiness or is life, after all, mere vanity?

Calvin answers: "It is not without good reason that David so frequently inculcates this doctrine, that the righteous are blessed because God provides for their necessities. We see how prone the minds of men are to distrust, and how much they are vexed by an excess of cares and anxieties from which they are unable to extricate themselves, while, on the other hand, they fall into another error in being more anxious regarding the future than there is any reason for; and yet, however active and industrious in the formation of their plans, they are often disappointed in their expectations, and not infrequently fail altogether of success. Nothing therefore, is more profitable for us than to have our eyes continually set upon the providence of God, which alone can best provide for us every thing we need."

Anxiety is overcome when after the manner of Jesus Christ we say, "Nevertheless not my will, but thine, be done" (Luke 22:42). Then we belong to God and he is given control over our lives, our surroundings and over all the things that might otherwise hurt us.

Prayer: O God, acquaint us anew with the realities which are eternal, and then we shall live confidently in an age of anxiety. In Christ's name. Amen.

PERSEVERANCE

Psalm 37:25 "I have been young, and now am old; yet I have not seen the righteous forsaken or his children begging bread."

Perseverance, Calvin held, is the gift of God. ". . . some persevere to the end, and others decline and fail in the midst of their course. For perseverance itself also is a gift of God, which he bestows not on all promiscuously, but imparts to whom he pleases."

The persevering man is often sorely tried. "We must also bear this in mind, that if God sometimes involves the faithful in the same punishments by which he takes vengeance upon the ungodly—seeing them, for example, affected with the same diseases—in doing so there is no inconsistence; for although they do not come the length of condemning God, nor are devoted to wickedness, nor even act according to their own inclination, nor yield themselves wholly to the influence of sin like the wicked, yet are they not free of all blame; and, therefore, it need not surprise us though they are sometimes subjected to temporal punishments. We are, however, certain of this, that God makes such provision for his own people, that, being contented with their lot, they are never in want; because, by living sparingly, they always have enough, as Paul says in Phillipians 4:12a, "I know how to be abased, and I know how to abound."

In dedicating the *Institutes of the Christian Religion* to King Francis of France, Calvin shows how the gift of perseverance sustains those under sore trial. The enemies of the reformers were trying to induce the king to persecute them. Calvin wrote to the King: ". . . if your ears are so preoccupied with the whispers of the malevolent, as to leave no opportunity for the accused to speak for themselves, and if those outrageous furies, with your connivance, continue to persecute with imprisonments, scourges, tortures, confiscations and flames, we shall indeed, like sheep destined to the slaughter, be reduced to the greatest extremities. Yet shall we in patience possess our souls, and wait for the mighty hand of the Lord, which undoubtedly will in time appear, and show itself armed for the deliverance of the poor from their affliction, and for the punishment of their despisers, who now exult in such perfect security."

Prayer: Give us, O Lord, the living root of faith that we may persevere valiantly unto the end and be exalted into the liberty of thine eternal kingdom. In Christ's name. Amen.

THANKSGIVING

Psalm 40:3a "He put a new song in my mouth, a song of praise to our God."

In the twilight of her years Madam Ernestine Schumann-Heink looked back over her full life. Although she had achieved fame and renown, she also had known much sorrow; yet she was able to say: "To live is to be thankful; to know night and day, and changing seasons, to hear golden laughter, and even to weep softly—just to be alive is to be thankful."

John Calvin would agree, with the additional stipulation that our thanksgiving is to be directed toward God. "In whatever way God is pleased to succor us, he asks nothing else from us in return but that we should be thankful for and remember it. As often, therefore, as he bestows benefits upon us, so often does he open our mouths to praise his name. . . ." Yet, Calvin does not stop there. In company with the Psalmist who sang, "He put a new song in my mouth, he goes on to affirm, ". . . the more mightily he stretches forth his hand to help us, the more does it become us to stir up ourselves to fervent zeal in this holy exercise, so that our songs may correspond to the greatness of the favor which has been conferred upon us."

Howard Thurman has caught the ecstasy of the thankful heart in these words: "There is the intimate sense of being upheld and cradled by strength that is not of our own making, something that gives to life a quality of integrity and meaning which we, of ourselves, could never generate; the gentle upheaval in the heart reminding us to lift up our heads and be of good courage."

Prayer: We wait upon thee, our Father, thankful that thy mercies are boundless and fit every situation. We especially rejoice in the gift of thy Son, Jesus Christ, who came to earth to put a new song in the heart. May we ever refresh ourselves at the living springs of thy grace, believing that we shall not be disappointed. In his name. Amen.

CROSS

Psalm 44:22 "Nay, for thy sake we are slain all the day long, and accounted as sheep for the slaughter."

"But whilst in his [God's] incomparable goodness he fully pardons all our sins, he yet allows us to be exposed to unmerited persecutions, that we may with greater alacrity glory in bearing the cross with Christ, and thereby become partakers with him in his blessed resurrection. . . .

"Thus, then, we ought to regard it as a settled point, that a state of continual warfare in bearing the cross is enjoined upon us by divine appointment. Sometimes, it is true, a truce or respite may be granted us; for God has compassion upon our infirmity: but although the sword of persecution is not always unsheathed against us, yet, as we are the members of Christ, it behooves us always to be ready to bear the cross with him. Lest, therefore, the severity of the cross should dismay us, let us always have present to our view this condition of the Church, that as we are adopted in Christ, we are appointed to the slaughter. If we neglect to do this, the same thing will befall us which happens to many apostates; for as it is in their judgment too severe and wretched a state, even while they live, to be continually dying, to be exposed to the mockery of other, and not to have one moment free from fear—to rid themselves of that necessity they shamefully forsake and deny Christ. In order, therefore, that weariness, or dread of the cross, may not root up from our hearts true godliness, let us continually reflect upon this, that it behooves us to drink the cup which God puts into our hands, and that no one can be a Christian who does not dedicate himself to God."

Prayer: O blessed Lord of Calvary, thy cross shows us that our goodness is not good enough. Yet in the power of thy cross we dare to believe that our dry bones can and will live. On thee, O Jesus, all our hopes depend. Amen.

WEALTH

Psalm 48:3 "Within her citadels God has shown himself a sure defense."

Emerson once said of money, "It costs too much." Calvin would concur. "Worldly wealth, from our natural perverseness, tends to dazzle our eyes, and to make us forget God. . . ." The love of money is the root of all evils (I Tim. 6:10) because it consumes too much energy, wastes too much time, distorts perspective, blunts moral senses, makes one indifferent to human suffering and closes the door on God.

"Therefore, we ought to meditate with special attention upon this doctrine, that whatever we possess, which seems worthy of being prized, must not be permitted to obscure the knowledge of the power and grace of God; but that, on the contrary, the glory of God ought always clearly to shine forth in all the gifts with which he may be pleased to bless and adorn us; so that we may account ourselves rich and happy in him, and no where else."

When we see ourselves as stewards of God in all the rich relationships of life, when our first purpose comes to be to do his will and live in intimate fellowship with him, then God becomes a living power in our lives. H. G. Wells wrote, "Until man has found God, and has been found by God, he begins at no beginning and works to no end. . . . Nothing in the universe or in man's life falls into place except with God; with God who fights with man and through man against everything that is evil; who loves men, and stands ready to use us in his immortal adventure against waste; disorder, cruelty, vice, blind force, nonexistence, everything that destroys. God is the end and the meaning of the universe, the only King. God's kingdom on earth is not a dream or an uncertain project, but the inevitable destiny of mankind."

Prayer: Help us, O God, to be honest with thee so that we may be honest. Keep before us the awareness that every possession is a trust from thee, and that in this life it is not what we take up but what we give up that makes us rich. Amen.

SCRIPTURE

Psalm 49:4a "I will incline my ear to a proverb."

Why read the Bible? Calvin held that ". . . there is such life energy in God's Word that it quickens the souls of all to whom God grants participation in it. The truths of revelation are so high as to exceed our comprehension; but, at the same time, the Holy Spirit has accommodated them so far to our capacity, as to render all Scripture profitable for instruction. None can plead ignorance: for the deepest and most difficult doctrines are made plain to the most simple and unlettered of mankind."

Bishop Paul B. Kern of the Methodist Church once gave these reasons for reading the Bible: "I read my Bible because (1) within its pages I find power for the ordering of my inner life; (2) it offers a way of escape from those inner perils which threaten our modern life; (3) in its pages are found the secrets by which men walk the pathways of light and hope and freedom; (4) it assures me that man is supremely dear to God; (5) it points the way to world brotherhood; (6) it tells me whither

I am bound and why; (7) it offers me sound social philosophy; (8) it teaches me, in the words of Emerson, that the lesson of life is to believe what the years and the centuries say, as against the hours."

But *how* should one read the Bible? Calvin replies, ". . . if we turn pure eyes and upright senses toward it, the majesty of God will immediately come to view, subdue our bold rejection, and compel us to obey."

Prayer: Fresh light shall yet break forth from thy written Word, O Lord. Kindle and renew our desire to read and ponder its meaning that we may find through it a faith superior to all opinion. In Jesus' name. Amen.

WORSHIP

Psalm 57:7 "My heart is steadfast, O God, . . . I will sing and make melody!"

The mode of worship is a recurring theme in Calvin's commentary on the Psalms. This is to be expected for the Psalms contain the liturgy of the temple worship, the meaning of which Calvin was trying to recapture for his readers. How does one worship God? Freely and eagerly, or stiffly and mechanically? Do we keenly anticipate the hour to be spent in the presence of the Most High and prepare our spirits accordingly? Calvin held that such planning was a part of the mode of worship and a necessary prerequisite to the effective praise of one's Creator.

"My heart is steadfast, O God! Some read *fixed*, or *confirmed*, and the Hebrew word *nacon*, bears that signification as well as the other. If we adopt it, we must understand David as saying that he had well and duly meditated upon the praises which he was about to offer; that he did not rush into a hurried and perfunctory discharge of this service, as too many are apt to do, but addressed himself to it with steadfast purpose of heart. . . . I prefer, however, the other translation, which bears that he was ready to enter upon the service with all cheerfulness and cordiality. And although, wherever this spirit is really felt, it will lead to steadfastness of religious exercise, it is not without importance that the reader should be apprised of the force of the word which is here employed in the Hebrew. The ready heart is here opposed by David to the mere lip service of the hypocrite, on the one hand, and to dead or sluggish service on the other. He addressed himself to this voluntary sacrifice with a sincere fervor of spirit, casting aside sloth, and whatever might prove a hindrance in the duty."

Prayer: God of our fathers, may we so solemnly, eagerly and earnestly yearn for thee, that when we enter thy courts we may surely find thee, whom to know is our highest joy. In Christ's name. Amen.

PRESERVATION

Psalm 60:11 "O grant us help against the foe, for vain is the help of man!"

It was said of the Puritans that they feared nothing but God. Thus they were nerved to face despotic monarchs, the savage wilderness and the assorted cares and trials of life with composure and tranquility. They knew the assurance Calvin expressed in these lines:

"God in accomplishing our preservation, may use the agency of man, but he reserves it to himself, as his peculiar prerogative, to deliver, and will not suffer them to rob him of his glory. The deliverance which comes to us in this manner through human agency must properly be ascribed to God. All that David meant to assert is, that such confidences as are not derived from God are worthless and vain. And to confirm this position, he declares in the last verse of the Psalm, that as, on the one hand, we can do nothing without him, so, on the other, we can do all things by his help."

Our age, prone to fear everything but God, would do well to make the Almighty more than an affiliate. The weakness of our religion and the impotence of the organized church to deal creatively with the defiant dilemmas of the day originates in our unwillingness to yield authority to the Holy One "who sits above the circle of the earth." (Isa. 40:22). We want him to sanction our prejudices and desires and become an adjunct in the battle of life. Unlike the Puritans who were convinced that where God is properly reverenced all things are possible, we thoughtlessly pass over the judgment of God, thereby failing to reverence him and so we are ignorant of his forgiving, renewing love. God is as willing to be as real today as he has ever been—but on his terms, not ours.

Prayer: Help us, O Lord, to accept thy program so that we may experience thy power and presence. In Christ's name. Amen.

CHURCH

Psalm 61:6 "Prolong the life of the king; may his years endure to all generations!"

In our time, the church is under heavy fire from her critics. It was in Calvin's day as well. Yet the Genevan reformer predicted that as David's kingdom had survived so would the church.

"Prolong the life of the king. David cannot be considered as using these words of gratulation with an exclusive reference to himself. It is true that he lived to an extreme old age, and died full of days, leaving the kingdom in a settled condition, and in the hands of his son, who succeeded him; but he did not exceed the period of one man's life, and the greater part of it was spent in continued dangers and anxieties. There can be no doubt, therefore, that the series of years, and even ages, of which he speaks, extends prospectively to the coming of Christ, it being the very condition of the kingdom, as I have often remarked, that God maintained them as one people under one head, or, when scattered, united them again. The same succession still subsists in reference to ourselves; Christ must be viewed as living in his members to the end of the world. To this Isaiah alludes, when he says, 'Who shall declare his generation or age?'—the words in which he predicts that the Church would survive through all ages, notwithstanding the incessant danger of destruction to which it is exposed through the attacks of its enemies, and the many storms assailing it. So here David foretells the uninterrupted succession of the kingdom down to the time of Christ."

In a day when much criticism is being leveled at it, let the church remember what it is and the One to whom it belongs. Never, even in the time of greatest darkness has its light gone out. Our Lord promised that nothing could overcome it. Let us claim that promise for our time. *Prayer: Help thy church, O God, to remember who it is and what it is— the visible body of Jesus Christ. Enliven the church with the life of Christ until his Spirit and his Power reside in it and flow through it in service. Amen.*

SILENCE

Psalm 62:1a "For God alone my soul waits in silence."

"We know that the Lord's people cannot always reach such a measure of composure as to be wholly exempt from distraction. They would wish to receive the word of the Lord with submission, and to be dumb under his correcting hand; but inordinate affections will take possession of their minds, and break in upon that peace which they might otherwise attain to in the exercise of faith and resignation. Hence the impatience we find in many; an impatience which they give vent to in the presence of God, and which is an occasion to themselves of much trouble and disquietude. . . .

"Satan had raised a tumult in his [David's] affections, and wrought a degree of impatience in his mind, which he now curbs; and he [David] expresses his resolution to be *silent*. The word implies a meek and submissive endurance of the cross. It expresses the opposite of that heat of spirit which would put us into a posture of resistance to God. The silence intended is, in short, that composed submission of the believer, in the exercise of which he acquiesces in the promises of God, gives place to his word, bows to his sovereignty, and suppresses every inward murmur of dissatisfaction. . . .

"The believer may be overthrown for a time; but as he is no sooner cast down than he is raised up again by God, he cannot properly be said to fall. He is supported by the Spirit of God, and is not therefore really prostrated and overcome."

Prayer: O Lord, help us to learn to rest that thou mayest operate in us. Let silence often fall upon us that we may find that renewal which is from above.

After we have been still before thee, draw us forth from thy presence strong and patient to do thy will. Throught Christ our Lord. Amen.

Psalm 65:4a "Blessed is he whom thou dost choose and bring near, to dwell in thy courts!"

The Bible asserts that God has called or chosen in Jesus Christ a special group of people to be the objects and channels of his grace to mankind. These special people were chosen, first as Israel and later as the New Israel or the church, simply because it was God's good pleasure to choose them. Calvin expressed the sheer grace of election in these words:

"The Church and chosen people of God being in possession of the promise of the remission of sins, he [the Psalmist] calls those blessed whom God has included within that number, and introduced into the enjoyment of such a distinguished privilege. His language intimates that the election did not at that time terminate upon all; for he insists upon it as the special prerogative of the Jews, that they had been chosen by God in preference to the other nations. Were it supposed that man could do anything to anticipate the grace of God, the election would cease to be with God himself, although the right and power of it are expressly ascribed to him. But the Jews had no excellency above others, except in the one point of having enjoyed the distinguishing favor of God. The middle wall of partition is now broken down, that the Gentiles might be called in. It is evident, however, that all are not alike called; and observation proves the ignorance of those who will assert that the grace of God is extended to all in common, without any choice exerted on his part. Can any reason be imagined why God should not call all alike, except it be that his sovereign election distinguishes some from others? Faith and prayer may be means for procuring us an interest in the grace of God; but the source whence it flows is not within but without us. There is a blessedness in exercising trust upon God, and embracing his promises—a blessedness experienced when, through faith in Christ the Mediator, we apprehend him as our Father, and direct our prayers to him in that character; but ere this faith and prayer can have any existence, it must be supposed that we who are estranged from God by nature have been brought near by an exercise of his favor. We are near him, not as having anticipated his grace, and come to him of ourselves, but because, in his condescension, he has stretched out his hand as far as hell itself to reach us. To speak more properly, he first elects us, and then testifies his love by calling us."

Prayer: Help us to realize anew, O God, that once thou hast called us in Jesus Christ thy Son, thou dost never forsake us. May we live as those called out by thee into the new fellowship of thy church, and ever demonstrate our belief that thou art for us. Amen.

ANGELS

Psalm 68:17 "With mighty chariotry, twice ten thousand, thousands upon thousands, [angels], the Lord came from Sinai into the holy place."

"For the most part, we are apt to undervalue the Divine presence, and therefore David presents us with a description fitted to exalt our thoughts of it. Owing to our unbelieving hearts, the least danger which occurs in the world weighs more with us than the power of God. We tremble under the slightest trials; for we forget or cherish low views of his omnipotence. To preserve us from this error, David directs us to the countless myriads of angels which are at his command—a circumstance, the consideration of which may well enable us to defy the evils which beset us. *Twice ten thousand* are spoken of; but it is a number designed to intimate to us that the armies of the living God, which he commissions for our help, are innumerable; and surely this should comfort us under the deadliest afflictions of this life."

What form do angels take today? Let James S. Stewart answer: "Well, for one thing, the strengthening angel is often some shining word out of the Book of God. . . . Sometimes the strengthening angel is a fellow-creature. Sometimes it is a friend. It is a fact to which many of us here would bear witness—that one way God has chosen to draw near to us has been through our contact with some human being who had the blessed faculty of turning our weakness into strength, ... But there is still a third way: For sometimes the angel is none other than the Lord Himself. It is Christ who appears to us, to strengthen us. Indeed, in a sense, it is always Christ. When some word from the Bible lays hold of me, it is not just a word out of a book; it is Christ acting on me through that word. When some friendship reinforces me, it is not just a touch of human kindness; I feel that Jesus of Nazareth has been passing by."

Prayer: Teach us daily, Our Father, that thou wilt keep vigil over us, take upon thyself our defense and so direct our ways that no harm will befall us. In Jesus' name. Amen.

REPUTATION

Psalm 69:5 "O God, thou knowest my folly; the wrongs I have done are not hidden from thee."

My friend was a carpenter by trade. He had little more than an elementary school education. He was self-instructed in his vocation. Yet, such was his integrity that learned and ignorant, wise and simple, young and old, great and small sought his counsel. Once I went to him anxious about how a certain action would be interpreted by others. He only said, "My friend, no one can make a liar out of you if you are not one already."

Calvin wrote, "It were indeed desirable that our integrity should also be acknowledged and approved of by men, and that not so much on our own account as for the edification of our brethren. But if, after we have done all in our power to make men form a favorable opinion respecting us, they misconstruct and pervert every good word which we utter, and every good action which we perform, we ought to maintain such greatness of mind as boldly to despise the world and all false accusers, resting contented with the judgment of God and with that alone; for those who are over anxious about maintaining their good name cannot but often experience fainting of heart. Let us be always ready to satisfy men; but if they refuse to listen to what we have to say in self-vindication, let us proceed in our course through evil report as well as good report, following the example of Paul in I Corinthians 4:5, where he fearlessly appeals to the judgment of God, 'who will bring to light the things now hidden in darkness.' "

Prayer: O God, give us a character upon which we may thoroughly depend so that before we attempt to do something we may be something. In Christ's name. Amen.

FAITH

Psalm 71:19 "Thy power and thy righteousness, O God, reach the high heavens. Thou who hast done great things, O God, who is like thee?"

It has been said that faith is reason in a courageous mood. Calvin would agree. ". . . We should force our way through every impediment by faith, and regard the power of God, which is well entitled to be so regarded, as superior to all obstacles." Just as one must believe that an inference is valid before he can begin his argument for its validity, so there must be the faith that God loves one before he is able to live life in scorn of consequences. Peter Berger writes, ". . . Child psychologists tell us there can be no maturation without the presence of this faith at the outset of the socialization process. Man's propensity for order is grounded in a faith or trust that, ultimately, reality is 'in order,' 'all right,' 'as it should be.' Needless to say, there is no empirical method by which this faith can be tested. To assert it is itself an act of faith."

Calvin held that one can believe only because God himself has empowered faith. "Finally, our sense of the goodness of God should extend so far as to ravish us with admiration; for thus it will come to pass that our minds, which are often distracted by an unholy disquietude, will respose upon God alone." It is grace which produces faith and empowers faith to bravery. The gospel is not that we are to trust God and so win his favor, but rather that God already loves us and therefore, we are to trust him. This is the mainspring of creative faith. "It requires us to put confidence in God, who being infinitely superior to us, will sometimes appear unreasonable to us but in whom, . . . confidence yields the results promised. . . . When you become a Christian, you are 'no longer faced with an argument which demands your assent, but with a Person who demands your confidence.' "

Prayer: Fill us, O God, with admiration for thy great goodness. When temptation to doubt thee arises, launch within us a crusade of faith so that we may move confidently into the unknown. Help us to enjoy what we believe and to act accordingly. In his name. Amen.

GOVERNMENT

Psalm 72:1a,4a "Give the king thy justice, O God, . . . May he defend the cause of the poor of the people."

Along with Luther, John Calvin believed in strong government, "Let laws and the administration of justice be taken away, and the consequence will be, that the more powerful a man is, he will be the more able to oppress his poor brethren. David, therefore, particularly mentions that the king will be the defender of those who can only be safe under the protection of the magistrate, and declares that he will be their avenger when they are made the victims of injustice and wrong. . . .

"But as the king cannot discharge the duty of succoring and defending the poor which David imposes upon him, unless he curb the wicked by authority and the power of the sword, it is very justly added in the end of the verse, that when righteousness reigns, *oppressors* or *extortioners will be broken in pieces*. It would be foolish to wait till they should give place of their own accord. They must be repressed by the sword, that their audacity and wickedness may be prevented from proceeding to greater lengths. It is therefore requisite for a king to be a man of wisdom, and resolutely prepared effectually to restrain the violent and injurious, that the rights of the meek and orderly may be preserved unimpaired. Thus none will be fit for governing a people but he who has learned to be rigorous when the case requires. . . . There is much truth in the old saying, that it is worse to live under a prince through whose lenity everything is lawful, than under a tyrant where there is no liberty at all."

It was George Washington who said, "The administration of justice is the firmest pillar of government."

Prayer: Judge eternal, throned in splendor, Lord of lords and King of kings, With thy living fire of judgment Purge this realm of bitter things: Solace all its wide dominion With the healing of Thy wings. Amen.

DOUBT

Psalm 74:12 "Yet God my King is from old, working salvation in the midst of the earth."

The path of faith is not always tranquil, smooth and steady. At times even the most ardent believers have difficulty in feeling that they are really in communion with God. Martin Luther once cried out, "Who has not known that awakening of a dark morning covered by the black blanket of the last ultimate doubt?" What shall we do when doubt enters in? Calvin answers: *"Yet God my King is from old.* In this verse, as we have often seen to be the case in other places, the people of God intermingle meditations with their prayers, thereby to acquire renewed vigor to their faith, and to stir up themselves to greater earnestness in the duty of prayer. We know how difficult it is to rise above all doubts, and boldly to persevere in a free and unrestrained course of prayer. Here, then, the faithful call to remembrance the proofs of God's mercy and working, by which he certified, through a continued series of ages, that he was the King and Protector of the people whom he had chosen. By this example we are taught, that as it is not enough to pray with the lips unless we also pray in faith, we ought always to remember the benefits by which God has given a confirmation of his fatherly love towards us, and should regard them as so many testimonies of his electing love."

It is wise counsel when one is inclined to waver to go back to the very best one has known of God and to hang on to that. There have been bright days in the past even if now darkness prevails. Trust those fine hours and take heart; God's blessing, though in a different guise is drawing nigh.

Prayer: Help us, O God, to recognize doubt as a consequence of the risk of faith. Teach us that humility which acknowledges that although one does not always know, nevertheless with thee all things are known. Lead us to make doubt an invitation to a pilgrimage—with thee. Amen.

EARTH

Psalm 75:3 "When the earth totters, and all its inhabitants, it is I who keep steady its pillars."

Although Calvin's scientific view was conditioned by the language, thought forms and literary fashion of his day and reflect, therefore, the viewpoints on life, history and the cosmos then current, his exalted view of the Creator back of the creation continues to be relevant to the space age. He wrote:

". . . Although the earth may be dissolved, God has the props or supports of it in his own hand. This verse (75:3) is connected with the preceding; for it confirms the truth that God in due time will manifest himself to be an impartial and righteous judge; it being an easy matter for him, although the whole fabric of the world were fallen into ruins, to rebuild it from its decayed materials. At the same time, I have no doubt that there is a reference to the actual state of things in the natural world. The earth occupies the lowest place in the celestial sphere, and yet instead of having foundations on which it is supported, is it not rather suspended in the midst of the air? Besides, since so many waters penetrate and pass through its veins, would it not be dissolved were it not established by the secret power of God? While, however, the prophet alluded to the natural state of the earth, he, nevertheless, rises higher, teaching us, that were the world even in ruins, it is in the power of God to re-establish it."

John Dow sums up the Calvinistic view as follows: "God made all things, and therefore, as everything is His framing, it must fulfill His purpose and depend on His activity alone, and that activity is for spiritual ends. . . . There can be no cessation of the divine interest in the objects of His creation. . . . The potter is forever at work fashioning and refashioning for use or beauty, for service or delight."

Prayer: Grant us the wisdom, O God, to see that this good earth exists because thou dost will it to be. In its beauty and vastness, sublimity and awfulness, order and disorder may we see thine own majesty and mystery and recognize that thou art in the process of causing all things to serve the purpose of thy love as seen in Jesus Christ, our Lord. Amen.

LUST

Psalm 78:18 "They tested God in their heart by demanding the food they craved."

It is sometimes supposed that John Calvin was a kill-joy, frowning upon the expression of the natural urges and drives of the human body. Calvin himself refutes this notion in the *Institutes:* "It may seem absurd to some that all desires by which man is by nature affected are so completely condemned—although they have been bestowed by God himself, the author of nature. To this I reply that we do not condemn those inclinations which God so engraved upon the character of man at his first creation, that they were eradicable only with humanity itself, but only those bold and unbridled impulses which contend against God's control."

Calvin did frown upon the tendency, so prevalent in our day, to excessively desire sensual experiences that gratify the appetites, that is, to luxuriate in food, dress and especially sex: "Whoever, undervaluing and despising the permission or license which He grants, gives full scope to his own intemperate lust, and desires more than is lawful, is said to tempt God. Such a man acts as if he would subject Him to his own caprice, or questioned whether He could do more than he is pleased really to do. God has power to accomplish whatever he wills;

and assuredly, the person who would separate the power of God from his will, or represent him as unable to do what he wills, does all he can to rend him in pieces. Those are chargeable with doing this, who are set upon trying whether he will grant more than he has given them permission to ask. That therefore, the lust of the flesh may not stir us up to tempt him, let us learn to impose a restraint upon our desires, and humbly to rest contented within the limits which are prescribed to us. If the flesh is allowed to indulge itself without control, we will not be satisfied with ordinary bread, but will often, and in many ways, murmur against God."

Prayer: Enable us, O God, to have fun as thy children, without becoming slaves to our fun. Make us pure in heart as was our Lord, that we may more clearly see thee. Amen.

HYPOCRISY

Psalm 78:36 "But they flattered him with their mouths; they lied to him with their tongues."

Hypocrisy is a word not often heard in conversation today, partly because it is somewhat archaic and partly because of a natural reticence to accuse another of a fault of which one may one's self be guilty. Yet as Calvin well knew—and psychologists are quick to affirm—hypocrisy cannot be ignored, whether it is old style, that is, trying to appear better than one is; or new style, that is, trying to appear worse than one is. For the hypocrite is the phony, the pretender, the sham, the unreal one, the straw-filled man.

Calvin described hypocrisy as follows: "This is well worthy of being noticed; for from it we learn, not only the duty incumbent upon us of guarding against that gross hypocrisy which consists in uttering with the tongue, before men, one thing, while we think a different thing in our hearts, but also that we ought to beware of a species of hypocrisy which is more hidden, and which consists in this, that the sinner, being constrained by fear, flatters God in a slavish manner, while yet, if he could, he would shun the judgment of God. The greater part of men are mortally smitten with this disease; for although the divine majesty extorts from them some kind of awe, yet it would be gratifying to them were the light of divine truth completely extinguished."

Calvin suggests that hyprocrisy may best be avoided by centering our lives on that which is real. "It is, therefore, not enough to yield an assent to the divine word, unless that assent is accompanied with true and pure affection, so that our hearts may not be double or divided."

Prayer: Almighty God, keep us from using thee to foster our own purpose. Help us to be means to thy ends. Lead us to begin and end each day with the quest for truth and be honest to follow where it leads, whatever the cost. In the name of him who is the truth, even Jesus Christ. Amen.

CEREMONY

Psalm 81:1 "Sing aloud to God our strength; shout for joy to the God of Jacob!"

What is the purpose of the service of worship? Calvin answers: "The service of God does not consist in indolence, nor in cold and empty ceremonies . . . [but] whenever true believers assemble together at the present day, the end which they ought to have in view is to employ themselves in the exercises of religion—to call to their remembrance the benefits which they have received from God—to make progress in the knowledge of his word—and to testify the oneness of their faith. Men only mock God by presenting to him vain and unprofitable ceremonies, unless the doctrine of faith go before, stirring them up to call upon God; and unless, also, the remembrance of his benefits furnish matter of praise. Yea, rather it is a profanation of his name, when people quench the light of divine truth, and satisfy themselves with performing mere outward service. Accordingly, the faithful are here not only enjoined to come together to the tabernacle, but are also taught the end for which they are to assemble there, which is, that the free and gracious covenant which God has made with them may be brought anew to their remembrance, for increasing their faith and piety,

44

that thus the benefits which they have received from him may be celebrated, and their hearts thereby moved to thanksgiving."

Dr. John C. Bennett once put it: "Worship in the church is an end in itself. . . . It is wrong to consider the actual fellowship that is realized in the church to be only a means to world peace or to a similar social objective. . . . It is wrong to think of the life of the faith within the church only as a means of morale for work in the world. Through this life of faith the person becomes reconciled to God, to that which is for him life's center."

Prayer: Keep us faithful in our worship of thee, O God, that having frequented thine altars to learn of thee, we may make thy ways known in all the relationships of life. In Jesus' name. Amen.

RECONCILIATION

Psalm 89:28 "My steadfast love I will keep for him for ever, and my covenant will stand firm for him."

Reconciliation is the bridging of the gap between man and God and man and man, occasioned by man's sinful estrangement and alienation. The good news the Christian faith conveys is that the gap was spanned when "The Word became flesh and dwelt among us" (John 1:14). Paul wrote, "God was in Christ reconciling the world to himself" (II Cor. 5:19). Reconciliation has been worked out by Jesus Christ and we enter into it by repentance and faith; but it remains Christ's work first and foremost. Calvin felt that the believer needed to remember the finality of God's part in reconciliation because, ". . . It sometimes happens that the faithful cast off the yoke of God, and break forth into sin in such a manner, as that the fear of God seems to be extinguished in them. . . . Thus David seemed, to outward appearance, to be wholly deprived of the Spirit of God, whom he prays to be restored to him. The reason why God leaves hope of pardon even for detestable and deadly transgressions is, that the enormity of our sins may not keep us back or hinder us from seeking reconciliation with him. . . .

Due care must indeed be taken lest, by too great forbearance, loose reins should be given to men to commit iniquity; but there is no less danger in an extreme degree of rigor. . . . Still, however, we must understand the passage as amounting to this, that although the faithful may not in every instance act in a manner worthy of the grace of God, and may therefore deserve to be rejected by him, yet he will be merciful to them, because remission of sins is an essential article promised in his covenant."

God is for us and he remains for us even when we are undeserving of his favor. The skeptic may scoff at this claim; but that does not alter its reality. Reconciliation has been effected. That is the gospel.

Prayer: O God, we are saved to serve. Make us good will ambassadors of thy reconciling love seen in its fullness in the cross. Hasten the day when men shall be bound to thee and through thee to one another in mutual understanding and love. In Christ's name. Amen.

DEPRAVITY

Psalm 95:8-9a "Harden not your hearts, as at Meribah, as on the day at Massah in the wilderness, when your fathers tested me, and put me to the proof."

A doctrine with which John Calvin has been most closely identified is total depravity. That emient theologian of yesteryear, Charles Hodge, defines it as follows: "By total depravity, is not meant that all men are equally wicked; nor that any man is as thoroughly corrupt as it is possible for a man to be; nor that men are destitute of all moral virtues. . . . Total depravity [is] the entire absence of holiness; the want of due apprehensions of the divine perfections, and of our relation to God as our Creator, Preserver, Benefactor, Governor, and Redeemer. There is common to all men a total alienation of the soul from God so that no unrenewed man either understands or seeks after God; no such man ever makes God his portion, or God's glory the end of his being. The apostasy from God is total or complete. All men worship and serve the creature rather than, and more than the Creator."

In the light of this understanding of the doctrine let us consider Calvin's own words on the matter: "We are to notice, in the first place, that all men's hearts are naturally hard and stony; for Scripture does not speak of this as a disease peculiar to a few, but characteristic in general of all mankind (Ezek. 36:26). It is an inbred pravity; still it is voluntary; we are not insensible in the same manner that stones are, and the man who will not suffer himself to be ruled by God's word, makes that heart, which was hard before, harder still, and is convinced as to his own sense and feeling of obstinacy. The consequence by no means follows from this, that softness of heart—a heart flexible indifferently in either direction is at our command. The will of man, through natural corruption, is wholly bent to evil; or, to speak more properly, is carried headlong into the commission of it. And yet every man, who disobeys God therein, hardens himself; for the blame of his wrong doing rests with none but himself."

Charles S. Hodge concludes: "All other grounds seem merged into this, for our Lord says, that men are condemned because they do not believe in the only begotten Son of God."

Prayer: O God, we find that when we want to do right we cannot do it. We do not do the good we want to do but do the evil we do not want. Who will deliver us from this body of death? Thanks be to thee through Jesus Christ our Lord. Amen.

SPECULATION

Psalm 103:8 "The Lord is merciful and gracious, slow to anger and abounding in steadfast love."

Calvin was not opposed to speculation as such. The contemplation of a subject, the reflective process, the thought necessary to arrive at a valid conclusion—these necessary manifestations of intellectual activity are very much in order so that man may use his mind to glorify God. "We see among all mankind that reason is proper to our nature; it distinguishes us from brute beasts. . . ."

It was with the purely speculative that Calvin took issue. Once he castigated idle curiosity as follows: "When a certain shameless fellow mockingly asked a pious old man what God had done before the creation of the world, the latter aptly countered that he had been building hell for the curious."

It is consistent with his position on the place of reason to read: "We see that whenever God is mentioned, the minds of men are perversely carried away to cold speculations, and fix their attention on things which can profit them nothing; while, in the meantime, they neglect those manifestations of his perfections which meet our eyes, and which afford a vivid reflection of his character. To whatever subjects men apply their minds, there is none from which they will derive greater advantage than from continual meditation on his wisdom, goodness, righteousness, and mercy; and especially the knowledge of his goodness is fitted both to build up our faith, and to illustrate his praises. . . . We have no worse fault than that devilish arrogance which robs God of his due praise, and which yet is so deeply rooted in us, that it cannot be easily eradicated."

Prayer: Take thou our minds, dear Lord, we humbly pray;
Give us the mind of Christ each passing day;
Teach us to know the truth that sets us free;
Grant us in all our thoughts to honor thee.   Amen.

WINE

Psalm 104:15a "And wine to gladden the heart of man, oil to make his face shine."

"And wine to gladden the heart of man. In these words we are taught, that God not only provides for men's necessity, and bestows upon them as much as is sufficient for the ordinary purposes of life, but that in his goodness he deals still more bountifully with them by cheering their hearts with wine and oil. . . .

"But as there is nothing to which we are more prone, than to abuse God's benefits by giving way to excess, the more bountiful he is toward men, the more ought they to take care not to pollute, by their intemperance, the abundance which is presented before them. Paul had therefore good reason for giving that prohibition (Rom. 13:14), "Make no provision for the flesh, to gratify its desires," for if we give full scope to the desires of the flesh, there will be no bounds. As God bountifully provides for us, so he has appointed a law of temperance, that each may voluntarily restrain himself in his abundance. He sends out oxen and asses into pastures, and they content themselves with a sufficiency; but while furnishing us with more than we need, he enjoins upon us an observance of the rules of moderation, that we may not voraciously devour his benefits; and in lavishing upon us a more abundant supply of good things than our necessities require, he puts our moderation to the test. The proper rule with respect to the use of bodily sustenance, is to partake of it that it may sustain, but not oppress us. . . .

". . . When men have been carefully taught to bridle their lust, it is important for them to know, that God permits them to enjoy pleasures in moderation, where there is the ability to provide them. . . . His [God's] fatherly kindness should be to us the best mistress to teach us moderation."

Prayer: Search me, O God, and know my heart!
Try me and know my thoughts!
And see if there be any wicked way in me,
And lead me in the way everlasting!
Amen. (Ps. 139:23-24)

FATE

Psalm 105:19 "Until what he had said came to pass the word of the Lord tested him."

There are those who equate Calvin's doctrine of election with fatalism. This is both an inaccurate and an unfortunate assumption. While fatalism holds that the activities of men are as rigidly ordained as the movements of the sun and stars, the scriptural doctrine of election holds that in calling man to be a child of his, God has liberated him from fate. Man is in the hands of the living God, not blind chance. Thus life is not a gigantic game of Russian roulette, but an exciting adventure to which

God has called man so that he may become a participant in the fulfillment of God's purposes. It is in this light that we understand the following comment of Calvin:

"What worldly men, who acknowledge not God to be the Governor of human affairs, call *fate*, the prophet distinguishes by a more appropriate name, terming it *word*, and the word of each man. Nor do I see any impropriety in using the French word *destinee*. When the Stoics dispute, or rather babble, about destiny, they not only involve themselves and the thing also of which they treat in intricate mazes, but, at the same time involve in perplexity an indubitable truth; for in imagining a concatenation of causes, they divest God of the government of the world. It is an impious invention so to link together causes, interwoven with each other, as that God himself should be tied to them. Our faith then ought to mount up to his secret counsel, by which, uncontrolled, he directs all things to their end. This passage also teaches us that God will continue the afflictions of the godly only until they are thereby thoroughly proved."

Prayer: O Lord, when dense clouds darken our sky and all of our senses are benumbed with fright, keep us from that despair which leads us to doubt thy concern for each one of us. Help us to know that as thou didst make thy creation, so thou wilt take care of it. In Jesus' name. Amen.

HONESTY

Psalm 106:3 "Blessed are they who observe justice, who do righteousness at all times!"

". . . We know, there is nothing but the mere shadow of righteousness, unless a man cordially devote himself to the practice of honesty. He [God] requires perseverance, too, that no one may imagine that he has discharged this duty properly, excepting he whose constant and continued aim it is to live righteously and justly. We behold not a few who have only an empty profession; others show some signs of virtue, but do not maintain a consistent course of conduct."

Dr. Harold B. Walker writes: "There is something vital and sustaining in the knowledge that in standing right even in isolation from the crowd we are surrounded by 'a vast cloud of witnesses' who walked alone and yet were not alone. In a commencement address, William H. Miller of Chicago, sounded a solid note. 'If you wind up lonely because you won't go along with the crowd,' said Miller, 'I extend some sympathy for your present loneliness, but I confess I feel only envy for the exciting life you have before you.' Inner integrity of spirit is exciting because it links us to what is deepest in the nature of reality. It gives us something dependable to strive for, something to live for and die for, something ultimately meaningful. We are . . . afraid when our lives are committed to nothing that challenges us to be. Character that is worthy of self-respect always is the consequence of commitment."

Dr. Ralph Sockman suggests that Matthew 5:8 should be translated "Blessed are they who are not double-minded, for they shall be admitted into the intimate presence of God." The honest man is sure of himself because he is sure of God.

Prayer: Keep us honest, O Lord, not because we are afraid of being caught if dishonest, or because conscience nudges us, but because we reverence thee and respect the expectations others have of us. In Jesus' name. Amen.

CHRIST

Psalm 110:2 "The Lord sends forth from Zion your mightly scepter. Rule in the midst of your foes!"

Calvin's sublime confidence in the adequacy of Jesus Christ as the "man for all seasons" is vividly expressed in this passage:

"What time, then, our minds are agitated by various commotions, let us learn confidently to repose on this support, that however much the world may rage against Christ, it will never be able to hurl him from the right hand of the Father. Moreover, as he does not reign on his own account, but for our salavation, we may rest assured that we will be protected and preserved from all ills under the guardianship of this invincible King. Doubtless our condition in this world is connected with many hardships; but as it is the will of God that Christ's kingdom should be encompassed with many enemies, and that too with the design of keeping us in a state of constant warfare, it becomes us to exercise patience and meekness; and assured of God's aid, boldly to set at nought the rage of the whole world."

Jesus Christ will continue to be the "man for all seasons," because (1) he is the clearest illustration of the life we want to live in society; (2) his is the type of loving self-sacrifice which must come into being if the good society is to be realized among men, and (3) he symbolizes to his followers the resources from beyond time and space man must have if he is to overcome the obstacles to the life of loving good will.

A Presbyterian ruling elder, Col. Edwin Aldrin took the bread and the cup of communion with him on his monumental journey to the moon. During the first meal there he partook of the Lord's Supper, thus symbolically showing that Jesus Christ is destined to be the Lord of time, space and eternity. Wise was Calvin to point out "That however much the world may rage against Christ, it will never to able to hurl him from the right hand of the father."

Prayer: O Lord, grant "that we may truly and from the heart turn to thee, and offer ourselves to thee as a sacrifice, that thou mayest govern us according to thy will, and so rule all our affections by thy Spirit, that we may through the whole of our life strive to glorify thy name, in Christ Jesus, thy Son our Lord. Amen."

ANGER

Psalm 119:139 "My zeal consumes me, because my foes forget thy words."

Our Lord knew and expressed anger. He was angry not at what affected himself but at what hurt others. Were he here in the flesh he might well lash out at those sins of omission and commission which supinely acquiesce in the maiming of people through poverty and hunger and which permit spending millions on armaments for war while tolerating festering slums which destroy dignity.

Calvin was being both true to the sensitive spirit of his Lord and relevant to our century when he wrote:

52

"My zeal consumes me. The Psalmist speaks of his persecutors, by whom it is certain he had been subjected to much trouble. But although they were virulent and cruel towards him, he avows that it was not so much his own private wrongs which offended him as the violation of God's law; yea rather, that he was so consumed with grief on that account as not to be affected at all with his own individual troubles. This is an example from which much profit may be derived. We are too tender and delicate in bearing wrongs; and hence it is that if we are but touched with a finger, we are instantly inflamed with anger, whilst at the same time we are but coldly affected at the most grievous offences committed against God. But if we are animated with the zeal that inspired the Prophet it will carry us away to another kind of sorrow, which will take entire possession of our souls."

"Anybody can become angry—that is easy," said Aristotle. "But to be angry with the right persons, and to the right degree, and at the right time, and for the right purpose, and in the right way—that is not within everybody's power and is not easy."

Prayer: O Lord, when we get touchy, irritable and hard to live with, visit us with thy presence that we may become more gentle and kind. Take from us the glum disposition and the petulant mood, that seeking first thy kingdom we may place the service of neighbor above self. In Jesus' name. Amen.

LAW

Psalm 119:165 *"Great peace have those who love thy law; nothing can make them stumble."*

John Calvin is sometimes thought of as being more sympathetic with the legalistic spirit of the Old Testament than with the spirit of grace of the New. It is true that his training as a French lawyer made him hold the law in high regard, yet, he realized that the law could not save. The law was preparatory, instructive and prophetic. Yet it brought nothing to perfection. It failed to bring man into a right relationship with God. The relation between law and grace is clearly portrayed in this passage:

"Great peace have those who love thy law. If we take the word *peace* for a prosperous or happy condition of life—a sense in which the

Hebrews often employ it—the word *stumble,* to correspond with it, will be used for *adversity;* as if it had been said, that those who love God's law shall continually prosper and retain their position, although the whole world should fall into ruins. But a different interpretation will be equally appropriate, namely, that they have great peace, because, being persuaded that both their persons and their life are acceptable to God, they calmly repose themselves on a good conscience. This tranquil state of conscience, this serenity of mind, is justly reckoned the chief point of a happy life, that is to say it is so, when it proceeds from God's being reconciled to us, and from his fatherly favor shining in our hearts. The Prophet justly teaches that we attain this peace from the love of the law; for whoever would make it to depend upon anything else, will be from time to time trembling at every little blast."

Christ did not add to the law; he restored to it its integrity by fulfilling its demands in a way that it itself could not do. Thus as Calvin himself says, "Now the gospel differs from the law in that it does not link righteousness to works but lodges it solely in God's mercy."

Prayer: Not the labors of my hands
can fulfill thy law's demands;
could my zeal no respite know,
could my tears forever flow,
all for sin could not atone;
thou must save, and thou alone. Amen.

CHILDREN

Psalm 127:3 "Lo, sons are a heritage from the Lord, the fruit of the womb a reward."

"The meaning then is, that children are not the fruit of chance, but that God, as it seems good to him, distributes to every man his share of them. . . .

"As the majority of children are not always a source of joy to their parents, a second favor of God is added, which is his forming the minds of children, and adorning them with an excellent disposition, and all kinds of virtues. Aristotle in his *Politics* very properly discusses the question whether the having of many children ought to be accounted among good things or no; and he decides it in the negative, unless there is added generosity or goodness of nature in the children themselves. And assuredly it would be a far happier lot of many to be without children, or barren, than to have a numerous offspring, proving to them only the cause of tears and groans. In order, then, to set forth this blessing of God—the having of offspring—in a clear light, Solomon commends a virtuous and generous disposition in children. The similitude introduced for this purpose is, that as it were with a bow and an arrow. This similitude might seem, at first sight, a little too harsh; but if it is examined somewhat more closely, its elegance will be readily admitted. The Prophet means that those who are without children are in a manner unarmed; for what else is it to be childless but to be solitary? It is no small gift of God for a man to be renewed in his posterity; for God then gives him new strength, that he who otherwise would straightway decay, may begin as it were to live a second time."

Prayer: O God, our Heavenly Father who didst send the Saviour as a little child, and who dost love all children as thine own; bless, we beseech thee all children with thy favor and protective care that they may grow in wisdom and in stature and in favor with thee and men. May they see thee as their loving Friend and glorious King and follow Jesus Christ as their Master and Lord. Finally bring them and all of us to thine eternal kingdom. Amen.

AMBITION

Psalm 131:1 "O Lord, my heart is not lifted up, my eyes are not raised too high; I do not occupy myself with things too great and too marvelous for me."

"His [David's] submission in such matters stands contrasted with the presumption of those who, without any call from God, hurry themselves into unwarrantable undertakings, and involve themselves in duties which properly belong to others; for so long as we have a clear call from God things cannot be said to be shut up or hidden from us, or too great for us, provided we stand ready for all obedience; and, on the other hand, those who yield themselves up to the influence of ambition will soon lose themselves in a labyrinth of perplexity. We see how God confounds the proud and boasted enterprises of the children of this world. They run the full course of their wild career, they turn the earth upside down at their pleasure, and put forth their hand in every direction; they are filled with complacency at the thought of their own talents and industry, and, in a moment, when all their plans have been fully formed, they are entirely overthrown, because there is no solidity in them. There are two different forms which the presumption of those takes who will not submit to be humble followers of God, but must needs run before him. Some rush forward with a reckless precipitancy, and seem as if they would build to the skies; others do not so openly exhibit the inordinateness of their desires, and slower in their movements, and cautiously calculate upon the future, and yet their presumption appears no less from the very fact, that, with a total oversight of God, as if heaven and earth were subject to them, they pass their decree as to what shall be done by them some ten or twenty years hereafter. These build, as it were, in the deep sea. . . . while those who, like David, submit themselves to God, keeping in their own sphere, moderate in their desires, will enjoy a life of tranquillity and assurance."

Prayer: O Lord, keep our ambition within due bounds. Save us from envy and jealousy, and keep us from bitterness when others are preferred before us. Forgive our greed and conceit, O Lord. Help us to know that even when we are overlooked there is still a use for our loyalty and talent. In Christ's name. Amen.

TEMPER

Psalm 141:3 "Set a guard over my mouth, O Lord, keep watch over the door of my lips!"

Louis Pasteur's biographer tells somewhere of the patience of the great French scientist. He would seldom raise his voice with the mistakes of his students, but chose rather to patiently work with them until they had finally mastered the problem at hand. One day Pasteur discovered the deceitfulness of a steward who had substituted an impure seed for a pure one for the sake of profit. Pasteur found out about it and it threw him into a memorable rage. The steward shrank under a thundering torrent of denunciation. When it was finally over and he could collect his battered wits, the only thing the steward could remember was that the great Pasteur never wanted to see his face again!

Being angry is not sinful, but losing one's temper may be destructive. This Calvin knew and so he wrote: "As David was liable to be hurt at the unbridled and unprincipled rage of his enemies so as to be tempted to act in a manner that might not be justifiable, he prays for divine direction, and not that he might be kept back from manual violence merely, but that his tongue might be restrained from venting reproach or words of complaint. Even persons of the most self-possessed temper, if unwarrantably injured, will sometimes proceed to make retaliation, through their resenting the unbecoming conduct of their enemies. David prays accordingly that his tongue might be restrained by the Lord from uttering any word which was out of joint."

Prayer: Help us to know, O God, that when we lose our temper we show our weakness. Keep our mouths from working faster than our minds. Grant us the wisdom to perceive that when we lose our temper we alienate reason also. Give us the mind of Christ each passing day. Amen.

FLATTERY

Psalm 141:5a "Let a good man strike or rebuke me in kindness, but let the oil of the wicked never anoint my head."

"However hot good men may be, and whatever severity of language they may employ in admonishing those who have erred, they are still actuated by the force of brotherly affection. Nay, the very severity is, in fact, occasioned by their holy anxiety and fear of their brother's safety. The righteous act mercifully under all this apparent sharpness and severity—as the wicked, on the other hand, act cruelly who censure only in a very gentle manner. . . . . The other rendering of the words, however, which I have adopted, is equally suitable—*let the righteous censure me, it shall be mercy, or I will reckon it a benefit, let him reprove me, this shall be precious ointment that will not hurt my head.* . . . That is, let not the wicked seduce me to destruction by their pleasing flatteries. . . . This would make the passage convey a fuller meaning, that while David was pliable and yielding in the matter of reproof, he fled from flattery as from the fatal songs of the Sirens. However sweet praise may be to the taste at first, everyone who lends an ear to flattery, drinks in a poison which will presently diffuse itself through the whole heart. Let us learn by David's example to reject all flatteries, prone as we are naturally to receive them, and to renounce waywardness and obstinacy, lest we should put away from us those corrections which are wholesome remedies for our vices."

Before Calvin, Ignatius, one of the early Christian fathers, warned against flattery as follows: ". . . God has granted me many an inspiration, but I keep my limits, lest boasting should be my undoing. For that I need most at this point is to be on my guard and not to heed flatterers. Those who tell me . . . they are my scourge. To be sure, I am ever so eager to be a martyr, but I do not know if I deserve to be. . . . What I need is gentleness by which the prince of this world is overthrown."

Prayer: *"Forbid it, Lord, that I should boast,*
Save in the death of Christ, my God:
All the vain things that charm me most,
I sacrifice them to his blood." Amen.

PRAISE

Psalm 150:1b; 3a "Praise God in his sanctuary. Praise him in his mighty firmament! Praise him with trumpet sound."

"That the majesty of God may be duly reverenced, the Psalmist represents him as presiding on his throne in the heavens . . . which are a mirror in which they may be seen. If we would have our minds kindled, then, to engage in this religious service, let us meditate upon his power and greatness, which will speedily dispel all such insensibility. Though our minds can never take in this immensity, the mere taste of it will deeply affect us. And God will not reject such praises as we offer according to our capacity.

"*Praise him with trumpet sound.* I do not insist upon the words in the Hebrew signifying the musical instruments; only let the reader remember that sundry different kinds are here mentioned, which were in use under the legal economy, the more forcibly to teach the children of God that they cannot apply themselves too diligently to the praises of God—as if he would enjoin them strenuously to bring to this service all their powers, and devote themselves wholly to it. Nor was it without reason that God under the law enjoined this multiplicity of songs, that he might lead men away from those vain and corrupt pleasures to which they are excessively addicted, to a holy and profitable joy. Our corrupt nature indulges in extra-ordinary liberties, many devising methods of gratification which are preposterous, while their highest satisfaction lies in suppressing all thoughts of God. This perverse disposition could only be corrected in the way of God's retaining a weak and ignorant people under many restraints, and constant exercises. The Psalmist, therefore, in exhorting believers to pour forth all their joy in the praises of God, enumerates, one upon another, all the musical instruments which were then in use, and reminds them that they ought all to be consecrated to the worship of God."

Prayer: We praise and bless thy glorious name, O Lord; for the mystery and majesty of existence, for the world of beauty around us, and for the sights and sounds of earth in which we behold the wonders of thy created order. For all that thou art to us and all that we may be to thee, we give thee thanks and praise thy hold name, through Jesus Christ our Lord. Amen.

Subject Index